# 100 Popular

## Gratitude and Motivational Quotes

The underlying meanings of these Quotes and how to apply them in your daily life

Copyright © 2020 Brenda Nathan

All rights reserved

No part of this publication may be reproduced, distributed or transmitted in any form or by any means, including photocopying, recording, or any other electronic or mechanical methods, without the prior written permission of the publisher.

ISBN: 978-1-952358-00-5

Limits of Liability and Disclaimer of Warranty

The author and publisher shall not be liable for your misuse of this material. This book is strictly for informational and educational purposes.

# CONTENTS

Introduction ........................................................................ 1

100 Popular Gratitude and Motivational Quotes ......... 3

Daily Practice .................................................................. 105

Other Books by Brenda Nathan ................................. 107

# INTRODUCTION

Gratitude is a feeling of appreciation for what one has. It is a feeling of thankfulness for the blessings we have received. Gratitude should be directed at everything we are creating in our life. I believe it is the foundation of our life. There is no joy without Gratitude. We cannot feel gratitude when we are angry or fearful. Cultivating an attitude of gratitude can truly change our life. Feeling gratitude in the present moment makes us happier and more relaxed, and improves our overall health and well-being.

Anything that we want to happen in our life needs to be practiced regularly. I believe a daily practice of writing down our gratitude can change our life.

Gratitude is the single most important tool that has made the most difference in my life. *100 Popular Gratitude and Motivational Quotes* is a book compiled with daily inspiration, gratitude, and joy in mind. These quotes have been curated to bring your dreams to the forefront of your mind and encourage you to be everything that you see for yourself.

I hope this book helps you in living a life of joy and abundance.

Thank you,

Brenda Nathan

# 100 Popular Gratitude and Motivational Quotes

# QUOTE 1

***Three grand essentials to happiness in this life are something to do, something to love, and something to hope for.***

***~ Joseph Addison*3**

Firstly, we always need a purpose to our life. We find inner happiness when we make progress in our life. We need to find something to do that makes us grow. This way we will feel energized. Secondly, Love is all around us. It is easy to find something or someone one to love if we pay attention. It is important to take a moment to notice the love around us and be appreciative. Thirdly, we need to have a dream. A dream that we are pursuing. A dream that by pursuing, we are growing. When we pursue our dream, we are continuously growing and this gives us energy and happiness.

## QUOTE 2

*Prayer should be the key of the day and the lock of the night.*

*~ George Herbert*

The more we communicate with God, the clearer we can make our destiny for ourselves. Throughout each day, we should be turning to prayer as a force for centering ourselves and becoming more grounded in the reality of the universe. Nothing is out of God' reach, so whatever challenges we are facing, we can always turn to God for answers and solutions.

## QUOTE 3

*The best preparation for tomorrow is to do today's work superbly well.*

*~ William Osler*

We must strive to live with purpose. When we live with purpose, we feel good inside. We all have our purpose. We are not going to find our purpose immediately. We must constantly experience things and eventually we will be in alignment with our source and we will know in our heart when we are living a life of purpose. When we are living a full life, we will be full of energy and will be ready for anything and everything.

# QUOTE 4

*Keep love in your heart. A life without it is like a sunless garden when the flowers are dead.*

*~ Oscar Wilde*

Love is what moves the world. We are love. Love is around us all the time if we can just take a moment to notice it. We need to take a moment to appreciate what is around us and not take it for granted. Are you feeling angry and frustrated because something did not work for you or something disappointed you? At all times, bring love to the forefront of all your experiences. Your actions must reflect the underlying love in your heart. If you act with love, you will not have regrets. You never want to have regrets in your life when you could have chosen to act with love and kindness to yourself and to others.

# QUOTE 5

*The future is purchased by the present.*

*~ Samuel Johnson*

Everything is happening to us in this moment. Our actions at this moment will influence what our life will be in the next moment and the next and so on. Our future is a culmination of our present moments. It is important to live in the present moment. Are you living an authentic life in the present moment? What is your current focus in your life? Where is your energy directed? Pay attention to the present moment. It is influencing your next moment and hence your future. You really are buying in to your future with your present moment.

# QUOTE 6

*Write it on your heart that every day is the best day in the year.*

*~ Ralph Waldo Emerson*

Optimism is more than just a good idea or a nice-sounding platitude: it's a necessity for living a happy and fulfilling life. Every day you wake up, remind yourself of what it is in your life you need to be grateful for. There is something amazing going on in your life, even at the times when it seems like you are facing more challenges than usual.

# QUOTE 7

## *The way to know life is to love many things.*

## *~ Vincent Van Gogh*

What we focus on in our life grows. Many times, we just focus on a few things and when one of those few things disappoint us or do not work for us, we are shattered. To live a full life, share your focus on many things and love many things. That means focus on relationships, personal development, career, children, health etc. Don't just focus on one thing. If you focus on many things and one thing does not work, this will only leave a small gap in your life. If you focus on fewer things and one thing disappoints you, you will have a massive hole in your life which you would need to be filled. Steer your focus on many things and love many things. You will be rewarded with different experiences which will create abundance and love for your life. Life is full of experiences. You can label them "good" or "bad" experiences. But they are simply experiences. If you can focus your life on many things, you will have many experiences which will expand your awareness and you can live a full live in awe and appreciation.

# QUOTE 8

## *Gratitude should be directed at everything in this life.*

### *~ Brenda Nathan*

Gratitude is a state of being. Gratitude should be the state you always want to be in. When you are in a state of gratitude, you feel a sense of fulfilment. A certain lightness to your life. A wholeness. Our state influences our perception of life. When our state is full of gratitude, we feel powerful and feel an alignment with our source. If we can feel gratitude at all times in our life, during happiness, sorrow, disappointments and joy, then we can experience these experiences in a way that would be in alignment with our true self. Fear keeps us locked up. Gratitude is a key that opens the lock. If you can live your life with an attitude of gratitude, you can create your own life story of abundance, peace and fulfilment.

# QUOTE 9

*Never lose an opportunity of seeing anything beautiful, for beauty is God's handwriting.*

*~ Ralph Waldo Emerson*

Take time every day to look around yourself and notice all you have to appreciate. Just by being alive, you have been given a tremendous gift. There is majesty in every corner of the world, and the more you take time to be aware of it, the richer your inner life will be. The world has been written in bright, stunning colors, and we would do well to see those colors for all they are.

# QUOTE 10

*No man's knowledge here can go beyond his experience.*

*~ John Locke*

We can learn more from doing something and experiencing the effects of it, rather than being taught about it. True learning and knowledge comes when we have experienced the situation ourselves. Experiences are feelings that we will be able to know only when we have done something that resulted in that experience. If someone explains an experience to us, it is not easy to understand it fully unless we have gone through the experience ourselves. Hence, we are limited in our knowledge on what we have experienced.

# QUOTE 11

*Let the beauty of what you love be what you do.*

*~ Rumi*

Whatever you do in your life, love what you do. When you do things that you love, you enjoy it much more and are happy. If you love what you do, then you will feel more energetic and you will feel the time pass very quickly. Always find something to be grateful for in your current situation. Some people know exactly what they want to do in their life and others may not. Finding your passion is about taking tiny steps on what you enjoy and finally following your passion when you have found exactly what you want to do in your life that makes you feel whole. There is always something to be thankful in your life – in relationships, children, career, finances, nature, friends, family or personal development.

# QUOTE 12

*We don't receive wisdom; we must discover it for ourselves after a journey that no one can take for us or spare us.*

*~ Marcel Proust*

Knowledge can be taught but wisdom comes through our experiences. It is through our experiences that we learn and truly begin to understand and appreciate the beauty of our life. No one can give us experiences. Experiences are truly gifts. Experiences should not be labeled as "good" or "bad", they are all experiences which we can truly learn from. Life is a journey full of experiences.

## QUOTE 13

### *The most wasted day of all is that on which we have not laughed.*

### *~ Nicolas Chamfort*

Smiling together, happy together, laughing together: this is the scene that gives birth to long-lived friendships. Why? Simple: there is nothing any of us can do or find that feels better than laughter. It's everything to us, as humans, and best of all, it's a habit that is infinitely sustainable. Keep laughing. Find new ways to laugh. Figure out your own sense of humor and give yourself the gift of levity repeatedly.

# QUOTE 14

*Just as our eyes need light in order to see, our minds need ideas in order to conceive.*

*~ Nicolas Malebranche*

Our mind needs constant stimulation. Our mind easily gets distracted when we keep doing the same thing over and over again. Our mind needs to be entertained with ideas. Surrounding ourselves with people where we can discuss new ideas is very stimulating for our brain. When our brain is entertained, we feel energized. Ideas are food for the brain. Our brain needs nourishment. Start doing something new every day and you will keep your brain stimulated! Our brain also needs a break from the norm in order to be creative. That means taking a vacation helps our mind. That is the reason that sometimes we are able to solve complex problems, which we have tried to solve before, during our downtime or during our break when we are just relaxed.

## QUOTE 15

***God gave us the gift of life; it is up to us to give ourselves the gift of living well.***

*~ Voltaire*

Always be grateful for what you have. If you cannot find one thing to be grateful for, then be grateful for the biggest gift in your life – your breath. Our life is God's beautiful gift to us. Live your life with love and kindness and enjoy every moment of your life.

# QUOTE 16

## *To the mind that is still, the whole universe surrenders.*

### *~ Lao Tzu*

We have this inner voice, our chatter box constantly talking to us. The chatterbox is fearful. The chatterbox is the one that undermines us. The one which says "you are not good enough", "you are a failure". It keeps us in a fearful state. We need to calm this inner fearful voice. Silence our chatterbox. This is done by taking "time out" from our daily routine and sitting in a quiet place and relaxing. You can either focus on nothing or an object such as a candle flame. Just sit in stillness and with self-awareness. When our mind is quiet, we get clarity. We will be aligned with our source with infinite possibilities.

## QUOTE 17

*Our prayers should be for blessings in general, for God knows best what is good for us.*

*~ Socrates*

We know that there is a higher power that guides us. We can ask this higher power to guide us anytime. Asking our higher power is praying. How we pray is a matter between us and our higher power. This is specific to individuals. However, when we do pray, it is better to ask for guidance in our prayer rather than be specific as to what exactly we want as the higher power knows that whatever we are experiencing is best for us. The higher power knows the overall picture that we cannot see for ourselves. We just need to trust this higher power, our source, to guide us in achieving the purpose that we are here for.

# QUOTE 18

***Seek not to understand that you may believe, but believe that you may understand.***

*~ Saint Augustine*

In today's world, we tend to try and understand something before we believe it. We need to have trust in our higher power, our source, that everything is happening for us. We need to have the belief that everything is happening perfectly. It really is happening perfectly for us. Live in appreciation of the perfection in our life and trust that we will one day come to understand the true purpose of the life we have served in this world.

# QUOTE 19

*This world is but a canvas to our imagination.*

*~ Henry David Thoreau*

We are capable of much more than we give ourselves credit. Those wild, out-there goals you thought up for yourself? There is almost definitely a way for you to reach them. Limitations are an illusion, and whatever you can dream, you can achieve. While we live in the real world, we have a tool that can tell us how to alter the world to our liking in enormous ways.

## QUOTE 20

*When the mind is thinking it is talking to itself.*

*~ Plato*

We are constantly thinking. It is important to know that our thoughts are powerful. Our thoughts are creating our intentions. Intentions can be powerful if they are combined with gratitude, as they tell our source exactly what we want right now. Intentions are a process by which we exercise our true powers as humans: intentions manifest only when we are living our life in gratitude and appreciation and stop expecting an outcome.

## QUOTE 21

### *Make it your habit not to be critical about small things.*

### *~ Edward Everett Hale*

Live a life of lightness and do not carry burdens. The burdens that we feel come from attachment to past pain and trauma, and anxiety and worries about the future. Always try and see the bigger picture and do not be judgmental about small things. It is better to love than be right. We must always trust our source that whatever happens to us, we will be fine.

## QUOTE 22

***There is only one way to happiness and that is to cease worrying about things which are beyond the power of our will.***

*~ Epictetus*

Happiness resides inside of all of us. We have the power to make ourselves happy. We also have the power to stop worrying about things that we cannot control. If you are in the midst of challenging situations, it is also important to surrender your worries. Use affirmations to shift your focus from worry to happiness. Affirmations are words that we consciously choose to say.

When we repeat affirmations, they get imprinted in our subconscious mind. If you are worried about your future or a specific thing in your life, surrendering your worry is a good way to feel free of the weight of carrying these issues in your heart. You need to let go of expectations for the outcome of your life, and be willing to be guided by the higher power. The higher power knows the best and easiest way to achieve your desires. Worrying is only blocking the path of your intuition's alignment with the powerful source. Worrying keeps us from living our life to the fullest. It keeps us away from what we are meant to be. Stop worrying about things you cannot control and surrender to new possibilities.

# QUOTE 23

## *To forget oneself is to be happy.*

### *~ Robert Louis Stevenson*

It is a fault unique to humans: because we can reflect on ourselves, we will more often than necessary or appropriate reflect on ourselves excessively. This leads to anxiety, depression, and many other problems. It is better to take your mind off your faults, your shortcomings, your responsibilities, and your goals and cultivate a mindset conducive to becoming your best possible self.

## QUOTE 24

*Trials teach us what we are; they dig up the soil, and let us see what we are made of.*

*~ Charles Spurgeon*

It is easier to align with our deeper self when we are facing challenges. This is because, when we get rid of ego and look beyond our bodies, we can feel our alignment to our higher self and our source. Challenges are our biggest teachers. Nothing teaches us more in life than challenges. They are the fastest way to find our authentic self. Our egoless spirit aligns with our higher self.

# QUOTE 25

*It is our attitude at the beginning of a difficult task which, more than anything else, will affect its successful outcome.*

*~ William James*

We all have a choice on how we feel at any given moment. When we feel everything and anything is possible, we are energized and we will strive to achieve our goals. How we feel influences the outcome of a task. How we feel about the task at the beginning influences how we approach the task. If we feel abundance and joy, we will embrace the opportunity given to experience something new with a task and will complete the task with a sense of fulfillment.

# QUOTE 26

*Creativity is not the finding of a thing, but the making something out of it after it is found.*

*~ James Russell Lowell*

Creativity is doing something new. Creativity needs passion and commitment. We are all naturally creative but we can learn new techniques that enhance our creativity. When we try new things, we feel energized, excited and happy. It allows us to find new opportunities for our growth. We can find purpose in our life by going through the process of viewing our world as exciting, as well as spending time exploring it.

## QUOTE 27

### *To every action there is always opposed an equal reaction.*

### *~ Isaac Newton*

Every action we take creates an equal and opposite reaction. We need to consider this in everything we do and everything we intend to do. If we push on anything, it will also push back at us. If we give something, it will return back to us. If we spread positivity around us, we will feel positive as well. If we are kind to others, kindness will return to us. Sometimes, it comes back right away, and other times it takes a while but it always comes back. This is the law of Karma. This law teaches us to be conscious of our actions and the effect on others. It is important for us to expand our awareness of the cause and effect of our actions so that we may choose to act with love and kindness in all circumstances.

## QUOTE 28

*Believe that life is worth living and your belief will help create the fact.*

*~ William James*

We are all living our own personal story and what we believe is the theme that guides our story. If we believe that life is an adventure, our natural state will be of excitement and contentment. It is important to always be aware that our mind is filtering our reality. Our reality will reflect what our underlying belief is. Our mind can easily filter our reality and make us see things as good or bad. It is important to be always aware of our belief and live an inspired life.

## QUOTE 29

### *The strongest principle of growth lies in the human choice.*

### *~ George Eliot*

We humans have free will. We are able to make conscious choices every day. We must choose to explore new possibilities so that we can continue to grow. We can choose who we want to be at any moment in time. We can choose to be grateful and live in appreciation at any moment. We have the power of choice to embrace a life of fulfilment.

## QUOTE 30

*Our happiness depends on wisdom all the way.*

*~ Sophocles*

Happiness, contrary to what some may believe, is not the result of ignorance but of a fuller level of awareness. As we learn about the world and learn how to navigate its systems, we can become more skilled at riding the waves of happiness and staying on top of them for longer periods of time. This is a unique type of wisdom, one we can accrue over time, only if we are attentive to our needs and to the needs of others.

# QUOTE 31

*The true method of knowledge is experiment.*

*~ William Blake*

Knowledge is best acquired when someone learns through their own exploration. It is by discovering our own answers to issues and questions that we truly acquire our knowledge. Our experiences are our greatest teachers.

## QUOTE 32

*Do not be in a hurry to succeed.
What would you have to live for afterwards?
Better make the horizon your goal; it will
always be ahead of you.*

*~ William Makepeace Thackeray*

The secret to happiness is continuous growth and progress. Learning never stops. Success is not a destination. It is the journey that counts. Set new goals every day. Expand your awareness on a physical and spiritual level.

## QUOTE 33

*To live is so startling it leaves little time for anything else.*

*~ Emily Dickinson*

When was the last time you stopped, looked around, and appreciated the world for what an intensely crazy place it is? Filled with such creatures, brimming with wonder, this giant rock we call our home is more astounding than any person will ever know. Just to look at it, though, we can get a sense of its breathtaking nature. It is just so amazing.

# QUOTE 34

## *All things are difficult before they are easy.*
## *~ Thomas Fuller*

Difficulty is a matter of opinion. When we start something new, it is always difficult at first as we have not done it before. However, it is by doing it that we learn and grow and it slowly becomes easy. If we are fearful of something, it is by doing that very thing that we fear that we can be fearless. It does not mean that fear will go away. It merely means that we know how to handle our fear and will still do it anyway.

# QUOTE 35

## *The key is to keep company only with people who uplift you, whose presence calls forth your best.*

### *~ Epictetus*

Always surround yourself with positive people who can lift you up. Negativity is contagious. If we surround ourselves with negative people, the negative energy that is transmitted from these people will influence our actions and thoughts. Soon, we will start transmitting negative energy to others as well. Surround yourself with people who are in alignment with the higher power and these people can be your guide to your source. Sometimes, we live a life that we don't show up as our true self, living in a disguise that we forget who we really are. It is important to be with an inner circle of people where you can be your true self and embrace a life of wonder and peace.

# QUOTE 36

## *The final proof of greatness lies in being able to endure criticism without resentment.*

### *~ Elbert Hubbard*

Criticism is just someone's opinion and their judgement. When we judge others, it is based on our own past conditioning. It is based on beliefs we hold. These beliefs may not serve us in reality but we hold on to these due to our past conditioning. We could also be judgmental or critical about ourselves. We may think we are good at this or bad at that because of what other people have told us or how we feel at a given time. We all make mistakes but these are lessons for us to experience life. If we are making mistakes, it only means that we are doing new things. It is important to expand our awareness to understand that we are perfect in every way and to not worry about other people's opinion of us.

## QUOTE 37

*Love is the joy of the good, the wonder of the wise, the amazement of the Gods.*

*~ Plato*

Everything good – that is everything good without exception – is a product of the love that is a gift from above. When we can overcome the self-doubt we all feel at times and turn to the love we know to be superior, we can do incredible things. Our ability to maintain joy in our lives is something to behold, and we should be expanding that ability.

# QUOTE 38

***Truly, it is in darkness that one finds the light, so when we are in sorrow, then this light is nearest of all to us.***

### ~ *Meister Eckhart*

Challenges can make us align with our deeper self. This is because, when we get rid of ego and look beyond our bodies, we can feel our alignment to our higher self and our source. We are surrounded by infinite possibilities and creativity. We just need to become aware of our physical, mental and emotional state. We need to be in the present moment rather than obsessing about the past or the future. It is in the present moment, right now that everything is happening.

# QUOTE 39

## *The things that we love tell us what we are.*

## *~ Thomas Aquinas*

We are attracted to things because of our thoughts. When we love something or someone, it is because we are attracted to it by our vibrations. It could also be that we want to subconsciously learn from the experience. Once we learn that experience, we are no longer attracted to it. What we love at any given moment in time is what we are aligned to at that moment. Something that is desirable to us at one point in time may not be desirable during another. It is important to embrace our divine grace and be grateful and love what we already have in order to live a life of joy and happiness.

# QUOTE 40

***You might not always get what you want, but you always get what you expect.***

*~ Charles Spurgeon*

Wanting and expecting are two different things. Wanting is wishing for something to happen whereas expecting is knowing that it will happen. Wanting keeps you in a state of wishing, while expectation is living a life of appreciation and trust in your higher power.

# QUOTE 41

*Ask me not what I have, but what I am.*

## ~ *Heinrich Heine*

There is this habit, especially of us living in the developed world, to try defining ourselves by the people around us, by the job we do, by our hobbies, by our interests, by anything but our true selves. This identity, however, is fleeting, and it represents neither our character nor our personality. Who we are runs much deeper than the money we earn or the social circles we construct for ourselves.

# QUOTE 42

*Nothing will ever be attempted if all possible objections must first be overcome.*

*~ Samuel Johnson*

Intuition guides us to the unknown. Intuition is our inner knowledge. Embrace your awareness and trust your intuition. Most problems and objections are external. If you feel in your heart that you absolutely want to do something, just do it. Sometimes the blockage or objections can be based on past conditioning. To breakthrough past conditioning, we need to be aligned and open to our natural state of infinite possibility and creativity.

## QUOTE 43

*There is nothing like a dream to create the future.*

*~ Victor Hugo*

Dreams are a mental image of what we want to happen in our life. When our mind thinks that it has what we are imagining, and we are feeling emotional about the images, it will attract dreams into our life. When we pursue our dream of reaching our goals, and see ourselves attaining our goals, we will achieve our goals as our thoughts and actions will be aligned with our higher power.

# QUOTE 44

*Meditation is the tongue of the soul and the language of our spirit.*

*~ Jeremy Taylor*

When we are still, we become fully aware of the present moment. Taking some time to meditate helps us to connect with our inner divine grace. Our mind plays tricks making us see our reality according to our past memories or fears about our future. Our mind filters our reality according to our fears, and our perception shifts to reflect those fears. A daily ritual of sitting quietly for few minutes a day just focusing on our breathing can shift our perceptions and change our story to live an inspired life.

# QUOTE 45

*Enthusiasm is the genius of sincerity and truth accomplishes no victories without it.*

*~ Edward G. Bulwer-Lytton*

You can be right all you want, but unless you're right in a way that makes people happy, it doesn't count for anything. As much as we like to think that our logical minds are the end-all-be-all, we are all guided by our emotions much more often. Happiness: that's what is attractive to people. Tell someone something they don't want to hear without a smile on your face and you can be certain of a bad reaction.

# QUOTE 46

*__Contentment consist not in adding more fuel, but in taking away some fire.__*

*~ Thomas Fuller*

Sometimes, the answer isn't pushing harder. Sometimes, the problem isn't that we haven't done enough. Rather, we may just need to relax. Take a breather. Kick back. By showing ourselves enough respect to calm down and let go of our stresses, we can do more long-term than we ever could by constantly going, going, going. There is nothing wrong with realizing when you are too exhausted to keep demanding more of yourself.

# QUOTE 47

*If there is no struggle, there is no progress.*

*~ Frederick Douglass*

We must continue to learn and grow. We must be in continuous pursuit to maximize the gifts given to us. We have come here for a purpose and we must fulfill our purpose. There are no boundaries to our potential. We must follow our intuition to embrace infinite possibilities and creativity.

# QUOTE 48

*Everyone thinks of changing the world, but no one thinks of changing himself.*

*~ Leo Tolstoy*

Change begins inside of us. Our view of the world is based on our beliefs and past conditioning. Everything is happening perfectly. We can learn from all of our experiences. There is always something to be grateful for. We just need to notice it and live in appreciation.

## QUOTE 49

***Don't judge each day by the harvest you reap but by the seeds that you plant.***

### *~ Robert Louis Stevenson*

Always keep planting seeds. Try and do something new every day. We can learn from all of our experiences. Learning never stops. Never judge yourself or others. Success and failure are just labels that we give to outcomes that we perceive from our beliefs and past conditioning.

## QUOTE 50

***All truths are easy to understand once they are discovered; the point is to discover them.***

### ~ *Galileo Galilei*

Truth always resonates with us. We have divine grace inside us. Sometimes, we could be so out of alignment with our source that we may not understand when truth is right in front of us. We may become identified with our outer personality and become separated from our inner guide. We must continue to explore within ourselves and be in alignment with our source. We must be wide awake and work on expanding our awareness.

## QUOTE 51

*Laughter is not a bad beginning for a friendship, and it is the best ending for one.*

*~ Henry Ward Beecher*

Friendships are true gifts in our life. Sometimes, we become so busy with our lives that we may not spend the time necessary to cultivate our friendships. Relationships are built on trust. We must also never judge others. Accepting a person as they are is the true gift we can give that person. Laugh at life and laugh with life. Surround yourself with people who can laugh with you. Embrace all of your relationships with lightness and awareness.

## QUOTE 52

*Once you make a decision, the universe conspires to make it happen.*

*~ Ralph Waldo Emerson*

Once you're aligned with your source, you tap into infinite possibility and creativity. Anything and everything is possible. Awareness is the key to keeping you aligned with the source. It is so easy to get distracted. It is so easy to give up when something doesn't happen in the way you want it to. Just trust in the higher power and your life will be whole.

# QUOTE 53

*Happiness resides not in possessions, and not in gold, happiness dwells in the soul.*

*~ Democritus*

The work we do, the money we earn, won't bring us true happiness. We may find, after spending all our time and energy trying to hit a certain number in our bank accounts or make enough to buy the house we want, that we are still unhappy. The reason? It comes down to our mindsets. Unless we have learned to appreciate the smallest things, we will not appreciate the big things.

## QUOTE 54

***If you do not change direction, you may end up where you are heading.***

### ~ *Lao Tzu*

The present moment is the most important moment. You can predict your future by what you are focusing on in the present moment. If you are stuck or spending your present moment fearful, your future will reflect this. What is your current physical, mental, and emotional state? If you can become self-aware and change your present state to your natural state of emotional balance and wholeness, your future will reflect your true self.

## QUOTE 55

### *Things do not change; we change.*

### *~ Henry David Thoreau*

Our perception of our outer reality is based on our beliefs and past conditioning. When our perceptions change, our life story changes as well. Self-awareness is the key to transforming our life. We don't have the power to change others, but we do have the power to change our self.

# QUOTE 56

*Nothing would be done at all if one waited until one could do it so well that no one could find fault with it.*

### ~ *John Henry Newman*

We learn by practice. We learn by doing something. We cannot master something unless we practice and become better at it. We can choose how we define ourselves. Other people's opinions should not concern us. We are the only ones who know our purpose. We should follow our intuition, which is a guide leading us to live a life of purpose. We should not wait to learn something. We should start now, taking tiny steps towards our goal.

# QUOTE 57

## *Good actions give strength to ourselves and inspire good actions in others.*

### *~ Plato*

When we are living a life aligned with our source, we will be energetic and inspired. We will radiate peace. We will have an attitude of gratitude. People who surround us will be influenced and inspired by us. It is important to surround our self with positive people because they influence our actions.

# QUOTE 58

### *It does not matter how slowly you go as long as you do not stop.*

### *~ Confucius*

We should not worry if we are taking tiny steps towards our goal as long as we are taking those steps. Life is a journey of experiences. It is easy to get distracted and out of balance. It is important to take care of our needs and expand our self-awareness. Everything is happening in the present moment. Instead of obsessing about the past or the future, take tiny steps towards your goal in the present moment.

# QUOTE 59

*The mountains are calling and I must go.*

*~ John Muir*

When something is pulling you forward, you must listen to it. You must trust your instincts. Each of us will be pushed this way and that by the world, but we know internally what is right for us. Maybe you need to climb a mountain. Maybe you need to sit down and write an essay. Maybe you need to sing a song. Your destiny is yours to discern.

## QUOTE 60

*Gratitude is the inward feeling of kindness received. Thankfulness is the natural impulse to express that feeling. Thanksgiving is the following of that impulse.*

*~ Henry Van Dyke*

Gratitude is appreciation for all that we have. It is saying thank you to all that we have been given. The biggest gift that we have been given is our breath. Expressing gratitude is embracing what we have, and living a life of joy and happiness. An attitude of gratitude is for all the experiences and all of the things that we have in our life. Thanksgiving is giving back what we have been given in our life. We can give back by just being our true self. When you are radiating peace and harmony, you can inspire others. We are enough when we show up as our true self.

## QUOTE 61

*Let us learn to appreciate there will be times when the trees will be bare, and look forward to the time when we may pick the fruit.*

*~Anton Chekhov*

There are always going to be challenges in our life. It is important to appreciate the challenges as lessons in our life. Challenges are our biggest teachers in life. When we are facing challenges, we should ask ourselves the question, "What is it that this challenge is teaching me?". We must trust in our higher power that all that is happening to us is happening for us. We can choose to be in appreciation of everything that is happening in our life with the knowledge that the time will come when we will see the bigger picture of our life.

# QUOTE 62

*Habit, if not resisted, soon becomes necessity.*

*~ Saint Augustine*

Habits are our subconscious behavior that we repeat over and over again. If we continue our habits, we will not notice them and will be on auto pilot while doing them. We will soon think these habits are necessary for us. Habits can only be changed though new decisions and choices. It is important to cultivate good habits. You can choose new habits and if you keep doing these habits, they will become part of your life.

## QUOTE 63

***He who would learn to fly one day must first learn to stand and walk and run and climb and dance; one cannot fly into flying.***

*~ Friedrich Nietzsche*

We achieve our goals when we make tiny steps towards them. If we wanted to follow our purpose or dreams, then we should start by working towards them. It will take time for us learn and grow. Every experience is a learning experience. It is important for us to trust in our higher power that we will eventually achieve what we want. We are surrounded by infinite possibilities and creativity. We just need to align ourselves to our source.

# QUOTE 64

***Miracles are not contrary to nature, but only contrary to what we know about nature.***

*~ Saint Augustine*

Miracles are happening around us, all the time. We notice the biggest miracles when we observe nature. Everything in nature happens in synchronicity. Miracles can be big or small. There are miracles every day. A miracle is something that happens that is extremely improbable. However, there are miracles in our own nature all the time. Be grateful for all of the miracles in your life. More miracles will come into your life when you are appreciative. Gratitude is giving thanks for this moment that our source has created for us. Your life will be transformed when you start noticing and appreciating all the miracles in your life.

# QUOTE 65

*The art of being happy lies in the power of extracting happiness from common things.*

*~ Henry Ward Beecher*

History is filled with tragic stories of people who became convinced that achieving this or conquering that would fill the emptiness inside them. The truth is, it is the simplest pleasures in life that will us happy. Something like a sunset: there, we can find a limitless source of pleasure and gratification if only we can take the time to stop and appreciate it.

# QUOTE 66

*Appreciation is a wonderful thing: It makes what is excellent in others belong to us as well.*

*~ Voltaire*

If you can spot all the things that make someone great, you can become more valuable to them and make them more valuable to you. Everyone in the world has something to offer, something that makes them worth being around. Exercise your eye for seeing these special things, and then once they become apparent to you, make a conscious effort to remember them. Remind yourself why you like every person in your life every time you're with them.

# QUOTE 67

***It's not what happens to you, but how you react to it that matters.***

### ~ *Epictetus*

Each one of us will encounter days that are tougher than the rest. These days may sneak up on us, or we may see them coming from miles away. Whatever the case, it is incumbent on us to put our character on display by reacting to the tough days in a way that we can be proud. Failure becomes insignificant when compared to our response to it.

# QUOTE 68

***The level of our success is limited only by our imagination and no act of kindness, however small, is ever wasted.***

*~ Aesop*

Imagination is a mental image of ideas and concepts. We react more emotionally to imagery, and feeling emotion is important in manifesting our desires. When our mind thinks that it has what we are imagining and we are feeling emotional about the images, it will attract them into our life. We attract what we imagine. Our outcome is limited by our imagination. Always show kindness to others. Be kind to yourself as well. Do not waste time being judgmental. When you practice kindness each day, you will have a joyful and contented life.

# QUOTE 69

*The pen is the tongue of the mind.*

*~ Horace*

Writing is the way that we formulate our actions. When we write down our thoughts, ideas, goals or even gratitude, it becomes transparent. There is clarity when we actually write things down.

# QUOTE 70

***Our greatest glory is not in never falling, but in rising every time we fall.***

### *~ Confucius*

When you fall down, you get up. If you make this a rule for yourself, you can keep pushing yourself and keep improving. We will all discover we are in something for which we have not prepared sufficiently. Do we back down? Hopefully not! Instead, we accept failure as the price of education, and we continue to do our best.

# QUOTE 71

## *What we achieve inwardly will change outer reality.*

### *~ Plutarch*

Change starts from the inside. Transformations start from the inside. Our transformation may be physical, mental, or spiritual. When we change from the inside, this influences all our actions and are reflected in the projection of ourselves on the outside. When we radiate peace inwardly, we radiate peace on the outside as well.

## QUOTE 72

### *To love oneself is the beginning of a lifelong romance.*

### *~ Oscar Wilde*

Your first relationship with the world isn't your relationship with your mother or your father, and it's not your relationship with your partner in life. Your first relationship is your relationship with yourself, and from that relationship, every other relationship springs forward. If you love yourself, you can offer love to others. If you don't, you can't.

# QUOTE 73

*Cheerfulness is the best promoter of health and is as friendly to the mind as to the body.*

*~ Joseph Addison*

Happiness is dependent on our physical, mental and emotional state. It is important to be aware of our state at any given moment. We can change our state in an instant by choosing to be aware of our thoughts and changing our physiology. All the pieces in our body and mind are interconnected. Live in harmony with yourself, and embrace a peaceful life of joy.

# QUOTE 74

*Gratitude is the secret to manifesting an amazing and abundant life.*

*~ Brenda Nathan*

Gratitude is appreciation for every moment in your life. It is a feeling of abundance. It is saying thank you for all that you have right now. Your gratitude should be directed towards everything that you are creating in this life. It is the foundation of your life and is integral to all your experiences. It is a state of mind that you need to feel before your desires can manifest into your reality. You need to start feeling gratitude as you set your intentions. Intentions are the starting point for fulfilling your dreams. Intentions can be powerful if they are combined with gratitude. Intentions are a process by which we exercise our true powers as humans: intentions manifest only when we are living our life in gratitude and appreciation and stop expecting an outcome. Hence, surrendering to the now in appreciation is a way for our dreams to manifest. Let go of your desires; live every minute doing things you enjoy, and trust that what you desire will happen – then it will appear in your life.

## QUOTE 75

*A single grateful thought toward heaven is the most perfect prayer.*

*~ Gotthold Ephraim Lessing*

Say thank you! When we were kids, the adults were always telling us this. Say thank you! It seemed like they were just teaching us manners, but they were showing us the path to joy. When you realize what you have to be grateful for, you are giving yourself two gifts: positivity and awareness. See what is going right in your life, so you can welcome more of it.

# QUOTE 76

*Everything has beauty, but not everyone sees it.*

*~ Confucius*

Everything has beauty in it. It is up to us to appreciate it. Everyone is beautiful inside. Everything that surrounds us is beautiful. But sometimes, we are so busy that we do not notice the beauty that surrounds us. Take a moment to appreciate all the people, nature and things that surrounds us. Be grateful that you have been given an opportunity to notice this beauty.

# QUOTE 77

## *Our life is what our thoughts make it.*

### *~ Marcus Aurelius*

Our thoughts are powerful. Our thoughts have energy. If our thoughts are negative and fearful, then our life reflects this. How are you feeling now? It is a reflection of your thoughts. Are your thoughts stuck in your past or wishing in the future? Or are you living in this moment, in the present. Do your thoughts feel love towards another person? We know when another person has loving thoughts towards us. There is this connection that comes from another being when we share these good thoughts. Everyone has fearful thoughts but it is important to change our state. To change our state, we need to replace those fearful thoughts with gratitude and joyful thoughts. It only takes a moment to change our thoughts. We have a choice. Being aware of our thoughts is the key to changing our state. If we live in a state of gratitude and joy, our life will reflect this.

## QUOTE 78

*God has two dwellings; one in heaven, and the other in a meek and thankful heart.*

*~ Izaak Walton*

The nature of God is intimately connected with life and death. When have you been humble? When have you been grateful? At these times, you have drawn closer to God and fallen into grace. This is evident from the results of gratitude and humility: they lead to good things because they are good things.

## QUOTE 79

*Nothing is a waste of time if you use the experience wisely.*

*~ Auguste Rodin*

Every experience is a learning experience. There is no experience that is a waste of time. It is important to think of our experiences as expanding our self-awareness. Never judge yourself or others. The more experiences we have, the more we begin to appreciate the wholeness of our life. Life is a gift. Our breath is the biggest gift we have. Consider all your experiences as gifts. Appreciate it with your full heart. Say "thank you" for all your experiences and learn from them and help others when they are in need as well. All experiences are better served when we have lived it. There is always something to learn from our experiences. Ask yourself, what is the purpose of this experience? Every experience has a purpose. Find the purpose, learn from it, move on and experience new things.

## QUOTE 80

*Know what you want to do, hold the thought firmly, and do every day what should be done, and every sunset will see you that much nearer to your goal.*

*~ Elbert Hubbard*

We must strive to live with purpose. When we live with purpose, we feel good inside. We should follow our purpose no matter the obstacles we may encounter. Every experience is a learning experience and we should continue to pursue our purpose. There are no boundaries to our potential. It is us that create these artificial boundaries. We should embrace abundance and infinite possibilities to be fulfilled.

## QUOTE 81

### *When unhappy, one doubts everything; when happy, one doubts nothing.*

### *~ Joseph Roux*

We should never forget the extent to which our moods are tied to our thoughts. Every idea we get, every motivation we have, it is all inextricably linked to the emotions we are feeling. We must remember this when we get seemingly irresistible urges: it's connected to a feeling, and it will pass soon enough, leaving us better able to decide for ourselves.

# QUOTE 82

*A loving heart is the beginning of all knowledge.*

*~ Thomas Carlyle*

The best things come from love, and knowledge is no exception. Every time we are approaching the world from a caring, giving place, we are bound to learn lessons that are positive and that helps us to move forward as people. It is love that sets the stage for the most wonderful discoveries and learning experiences, so we should be cultivating love within ourselves constantly.

# QUOTE 83

*He who lives in harmony with himself lives in harmony with the universe.*

*~ Marcus Aurelius*

We need to strive to be in our natural state of balance. We are whole and our true self lives in harmony with our source. We are all interconnected. It is important to expand our awareness to live in a joyful and appreciative state of mind.

# QUOTE 84

***We are what we repeatedly do. Excellence, then, is not an act, but a habit.***

### *~ Aristotle*

We master something by doing it over and over again. We learn, truly learn, by repetition. Study your habits if you want to make a change in your life. Good habits that we have made can transform our life. A habit of writing down things you are grateful about can transform your state of mind in to a state of abundance and turn your ordinary moments into blessings. When you write your words on paper, they are much more transparent and can have a more powerful and lasting effect. You can also read and re-read what you have written down. Anything you make a ritual will eventually become part of your life.

## QUOTE 85

*The most certain sign of wisdom is cheerfulness.*

*~ Michel de Montaigne*

"Don't worry, be happy!" These lyrics seem simple on the surface, but they succinctly communicate one of the most elusive and one of the most valuable pieces of wisdom any person can obtain. If you can figure out how to be happy and stay happy, you can do something most people never will do. Keep a smile, a genuine smile, on your face, and you'll become someone that other people rightfully turn to for guidance.

# QUOTE 86

### *The art of being wise is the art of knowing what to overlook.*

### *~ William James*

It is so easy to get distracted with minor things that we can stop seeing the bigger picture. We can easily become stuck by focusing on things that don't matter. It is important to be aware of what you are focusing on and if they do not matter, it is best to overlook them and keep pursuing a life of joy and happiness.

## QUOTE 87

*Always laugh when you can. It is cheap medicine.*

*~ Lord Byron*

The pathway to long-lasting happiness costs nothing to travel. All you need is a good joke, a funny situation, or a friend who gets you. If you can laugh, if you can smile, you can overcome even the most wretched circumstances. Laughter is something everyone can share, and it costs nothing. It is in that way wholly unique: nothing is cheaper and nothing is more fulfilling than a hearty laugh.

# QUOTE 88

*Our opportunities to do good are our talents.*

*~ Cotton Mather*

Every one of us is born with our own individual talents. We all have a purpose here. Life is a beautiful gift. When we do good, we are fulfilling our purpose. When we maximize our potential, we are thanking our higher power of all that has been given to us.

# QUOTE 89

*You must accept the truth from whatever source it comes.*

*~ Maimonides*

Inside all of us is divine grace. When we see, or hear, the truth the divine grace inside of us will recognize it. It will make total sense. Truth always resonates with us because we have divine grace inside each of us. When something resonates with us, we become separated from our personality for a moment. We are in the space that is our natural state of harmony.

# QUOTE 90

*Thank God every morning when you get up that you have something to do that day, which must be done, whether you like it or not.*

*~ James Russell Lowell*

Our life is our biggest gift to us, the secret to happiness, to continued growth, and progress. Be grateful for all you have in your life. Every day is a miracle in our life. Embrace your wholeness and cultivate an attitude of gratitude.

## QUOTE 91

*There is nothing on this earth more to be prized than true friendship.*

### ~ Thomas Aquinas

Your friends are the people on your side. They will stand by you when the going gets tough and make sure other people recognize how incredible you are. The value here ought to require no explanation, but far too frequently, we fail to remember what a gift friendship is. Take time each day to remind yourself of the people you should be grateful for.

## QUOTE 92

*That man is a success who has lived well, laughed often and loved much.*

*~ Robert Louis Stevenson*

Money, power, fame. We worship them, but it is those among us who see the value of laughter and love who have achieved something truly worth mimicking. Every time you tell you a joke, you're creating something that makes life better. The relationships you commit yourself to maintaining, you should prize those above all else and recognize that your loved ones are the sweetest part of each day.

# QUOTE 93

## *It is never too late to be what you might have been.*

### *~ George Eliot*

You can choose to be who you want to be anytime. You become what you think. It is never too late to become aware of your thoughts and align yourself with your higher power. Start appreciating your ordinary moments and turn them into blessings by being grateful for this present moment.

## QUOTE 94

***We consume our tomorrows fretting about our yesterdays.***

*~ Persius*

We must live in the present. It is easy to get distracted with our past trauma and worries. Everything that we need is in the present. Everything is happening in this very moment. Don't waste a minute worrying about the past or obsessing about the future. It is easy to get stuck. Free yourself by becoming more aware of your thoughts.

# QUOTE 95

*Our best successes often come after our greatest disappointments.*

*~ Henry Ward Beecher*

Keep trying! It is a common story: this person or that one failed again and again, only to succeed at long last. The same thing could happen to you. Even when things seem hopeless, keep your head up and be consistent in your effort. Be steadfast; opportunity could be lurking around the corner.

# QUOTE 96

*After a storm comes a calm.*

*~ Matthew Henry*

There is always a period of peace after an upheaval. The peace comes from our own alignment with our source that everything is happening perfectly. We know from our inner higher power there is a purpose to all our experiences, and we can accept these experiences as gifts. When faced with problems in our life, we should ask guidance from our higher power within us, a guide that is always present and willing to guide us.

# QUOTE 97

*A thousand words will not leave so deep an impression as one deed.*

*~ Henrik Ibsen*

By our action, we can help and support one another. Practice kindness to yourself and others. You always feel good when you do something for yourself or others. Giving always makes us happy. When we give without expectations, we align ourselves with our higher power.

## QUOTE 98

*Creativity is not the finding of a thing, but the making something out of it after it is found.*

*~ James Russell Lowell*

Anyone can stumble upon a new discovery. When we put a lot of work into our discoveries, they become worthy of praise, but the modifications and tools we develop out of discoveries indicate a higher intelligence. When we respond to our discoveries with vigor and an open mind, we are doing the word "creativity" a service.

# QUOTE 99

*Genius is the ability to renew one's emotions in daily experience.*

*~ Paul Cezanne*

It is easy to get out of balance with our day to day experiences. We must become aware of our emotions. We must live in harmony with ourselves. Self-awareness must be practiced constantly.

# QUOTE 100

***Good actions give strength to ourselves and inspire good actions in others.***

### ~ *Plato*

Good leads to more good. As we cultivate positivity in our lives, we attract more of it. As we inspire others to do the same, we can create a massive, exponential chain reaction that means the difference between a happy existence and an unhappy one. Our lives are ours to build, and if we want to build them well, we must know the impact we are making on the people and environments around us.

# Daily Practice

I believe a daily ritual of writing down two to five things we are grateful for, can change our life. Gratitude makes us more optimistic and compassionate. True happiness lies within us. By keeping a record of your gratitude in a journal or a book, you will store positive energy, gain clarity in your life, and have greater control of your thoughts and emotions.

# Other Books by Brenda Nathan

The One-Minute Gratitude Journal

Daily Journal: A Powerful Habit to a Bigger Life

Affirmations & Creative Visualization: A 365-Day Workbook for Lasting Change

Gratitude Planner Joy: 52 Week Daily Planner Filled with Inspirational Quotes

www.ingramcontent.com/pod-product-compliance
Lightning Source LLC
Chambersburg PA
CBHW050329120526
44592CB00014B/2107